SCANDALS AND GLORY
Politics in the 1800s

DAILY LIFE IN AMERICA IN THE 1800s

SCANDALS AND GLORY
Politics in the 1800s

by
Zachary Chastain

Mason Crest Publishers

MASON CREST PUBLISHERS INC.
370 Reed Road
Broomall, Pennsylvania 19008
(866)MCP-BOOK (toll free)
www.masoncrest.com

First Printing
9 8 7 6 5 4 3 2 1

Library of Congress Cataloging-in-Publication Data

Chastain, Zachary.
  Scandals and glory : politics in the 1800s / by Zachary Chastain.
     p. cm. — (Daily life in America in the 1800s)
  Includes bibliographical references and index.
  ISBN 978-1-4222-1787-0 (hardcover)   ISBN (series) 978-1-4222-1774-0
  ISBN 978-1-4222-1860-0 (pbk.)   ISBN (pbk series) 978-1-4222-1847-1
  1. United States—Politics and government—19th century—Juvenile literature. 2. United States—Territorial expansion—Juvenile literature. 3. United States—History—19th century—Juvenile literature. I. Title.
  E337.5.C47 2011
  973.5—dc22
                              2010011421

Produced by Harding House Publishing Service, Inc.
www.hardinghousepages.com
Interior Design by MK Bassett-Harvey.
Cover design by Torque Advertising + Design.
Printed in USA by Bang Printing.

Contents

Introduction

History can too often seem a parade of distant figures whose lives have no connection to our own. It need not be this way, for if we explore the history of the games people play, the food they eat, the ways they transport themselves, how they worship and go to war—activities common to all generations—we close the gap between past and present. Since the 1960s, historians have learned vast amounts about daily life in earlier periods. This superb series brings us the fruits of that research, thereby making meaningful the lives of those who have gone before.

The authors' vivid, fascinating descriptions invite young readers to journey into a past that is simultaneously strange and familiar. The 1800s were different, but, because they experienced the beginnings of the same baffling modernity were are still dealing with today, they are also similar. This was the moment when millennia of agrarian existence gave way to a new urban, industrial era. Many of the things we take for granted, such as speed of transportation and communication, bewildered those who were the first to behold the steam train and the telegraph. Young readers will be interested to learn that growing up then was no less confusing and difficult then than it is now, that people were no more in agreement on matters of religion, marriage, and family then than they are now.

We are still working through the problems of modernity, such as environmental degradation, that people in the nineteenth century experienced for the first time. Because they met the challenges with admirable ingenuity, we can learn much from them. They left behind a treasure trove of alternative living arrangements, cultures, entertainments, technologies, even diets that are even more relevant today. Students cannot help but be intrigued, not just by the technological ingenuity of those times, but by the courage of people who forged new frontiers, experimented with ideas and social arrangements. They will be surprised by the degree to which young people were engaged in the great events of the time, and how women joined men in the great adventures of the day.

When history is viewed, as it is here, from the bottom up, it becomes clear just how much modern America owes to the genius of ordinary people, to the labor of slaves and immigrants, to women as well as men, to both young people and adults. Focused on home and family life, books in this series provide insight into how much of history is made within the intimate spaces of private life rather than in the remote precincts of public power. The 1800s were the era of the self-made man and women, but also of the self-made communities. The past offers us a plethora of heroes and heroines together with examples of extraordinary collective action from the Underground Railway to the creation of the American trade union movement. There is scarcely an immigrant or ethic organization in America today that does not trace its origins to the nineteenth century.

This series is exceptionally well illustrated. Students will be fascinated by the images of both rural and urban life; and they will be able to find people their own age in these marvelous depictions of play as well as work. History is best when it engages our imagination, draws us out of our own time into another era, allowing us to return to the present with new perspectives on ourselves. My first engagement with the history of daily life came in sixth grade when my teacher, Mrs. Polster, had us do special projects on the history of the nearby Erie Canal. For the first time, history became real to me. It has remained my passion and my compass ever since.

The value of this series is that it opens up a dialogue with a past that is by no means dead and gone but lives on in every dimension of our daily lives. When history texts focus exclusively on political events, they invariably produce a sense of distance. This series creates the opposite effect by encouraging students to see themselves in the flow of history. In revealing the degree to which people in the past made their own history, students are encouraged to imagine themselves as being history-makers in their own right. The realization that history is not something apart from ourselves, a parade that passes us by, but rather an ongoing pageant in which we are all participants, is both exhilarating and liberating, one that connects our present not just with the past but also to a future we are responsible for shaping.

—*Dr. John Gillis, Rutgers University Professor of History Emeritus*

Part I
The Birth of American Politics:
1800–1850

1800

1800 The Library of Congress is established.

1801

1801 Thomas Jefferson is elected as the third President of the United States.

1803

1803 Louisiana Purchase—The United States purchases land from France and begins westward exploration.

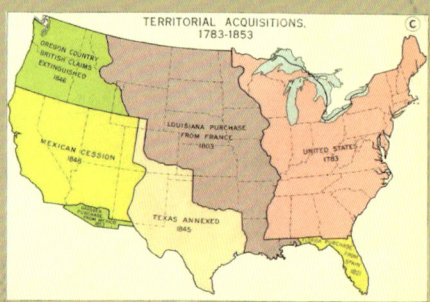

TERRITORIAL ACQUISITIONS. 1783-1853

1817

1817 James Monroe becomes the fifth President.

1820

1820 Missouri Compromise— Agreement passes between pro-slavery and abolitionist groups. It states that all the Louisiana Purchase territory north of the southern boundary of Missouri (except for Missouri) will be free states, and the territory south of that line will be slave.

1823

1823 Monroe Doctrine—States that any efforts made by Europe to colonize or interfere with land owned by the United States will be viewed as aggression and require military intervention.

1804

1804 Journey of Lewis and Clark— Lewis and Clark lead a team of explorers westward to the Columbia River in Oregon

1809

1809 James Madison becomes the fourth President.

1812

1812 War of 1812— Fought between the United States and the United Kingdom

of the 1800s

1825

1825 The Erie Canal is completed— This allows direct transportation between the Great Lakes and the Atlantic Ocean.

1825 John Quincy Adams becomes the sixth President.

1828

1828 The Democratic Party is organized.

1829

1829 Andrew Jackson is elected as the seventh President.

What Is Politics?

"Politics" is the process by which groups of people make decisions. We hear a lot about politics in our world today. Politics make headline news. People argue about politics. It's not easy for groups to come to an agreement, so it's no wonder that politics are often sources of tension.

For most of America's history, two groups, known as parties, have dominated the political system. At the beginning of the nineteenth century, the first two political parties had just been born.

Each side was concerned with how the new government should be organized. The Federalists believed in a strong central government. They were also in favor of industrialization, a national bank, and government aid to build roads and canals. The Anti-Federalists—who eventually came to be called the Democratic-Republican Party—held the opposite views: they were in favor of states' rights rather than a strong national government. They opposed a national bank, and they favored farming over manufacturing. They were firmly against the government helping to advance industrialization by building roads and canals. Supporters for the Federalist Party were mostly city-dwellers, merchants, and bankers who wanted to make money more easily. The Anti-Federalists were often farmers who lived in the country.

Duel

Hamilton

Burr

July 11, 1804

EXTRA! EXTRA!

Politics Turns Deadly
New York, July 13, 1804

Former Secretary of State Alexander Hamilton died yesterday from wounds he fought on July 11 with his long-time political opponent, Vice President Aaron Burr. Readers will recall that in 1800, Mr. Hamilton tried to prevent President Adams's reelection by circulating a private attack that Mr. Burr, long at odds with Mr. Hamilton, obtained and published publically. When Mr. Jefferson and Mr. Burr both defeated Mr. Adams but received an equal

number of electoral votes, Mr. Hamilton persuaded the Federalists in the House of Representatives to choose President Jefferson. Earlier this year, Mr. Hamilton opposed Mr. Burr's candidacy for governor of New York. This affront, coupled with his demeaning remarks questioning Vice President Burr's character, led Mr. Burr to challenge Mr. Hamilton to a duel.

The duel was fought at dawn on the west bank of the Hudson River on a rocky ledge in Weehawken, New Jersey. The Vice President shot Mr. Hamilton, while Mr. Hamilton's shot broke a tree branch directly above Mr. Burr's head. Neither of the seconds at the dual, Mr. Pendleton or Mr. Van Ness, could determine who fired first. Soon after, they measured and triangulated the shooting, but could not determine from which angle Mr. Hamilton fired. Mr. Burr's shot, however, hit Hamilton in the lower abdomen above the right hip.

Mr. Hamilton knew himself to have been mortally wounded. He was ferried back to New York, where his family and friends did their best to console him during his last hours.

Jefferson's America

At the beginning of the nineteenth century, many Americans felt the new government had become too strong and too involved in the lives of its people. In 1801, Thomas Jefferson was elected president under the Democratic-Republican party. When Jefferson came into office, he did so with the understanding that the government needed to return power to the states and their people. Jefferson served two terms and enjoyed enormous popularity, in large part because people saw him as a representative of American ideals.

But Jefferson's presidency also did much to increase America's power as a nation, especially by expanding U.S. territory through the acquisition of a massive piece of land called the Louisiana Purchase. Jefferson negotiated the purchase of this land from France in 1803. At the time, Jefferson's major

The Louisiana Purchase nearly doubled the size of the United States as it existed in 1803.

INCREDIBLE INDIVIDUAL
Thomas Jefferson

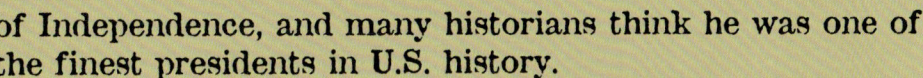

Thomas Jefferson was born in 1743 and died in 1826. During his lifetime, he served as the wartime governor of Virginia, the first United States Secretary of State, the second Vice President, and the third President of the United States. In addition, he is considered the primary author of the Declaration of Independence, and many historians think he was one of the finest presidents in U.S. history.

Perhaps Jefferson's greatest contributions as a politician, however, were his ideas: by putting his words to the Declaration of Independence, Jefferson shaped the way our nation thought about itself. He wrote convincingly about a democracy that depended on the well-being of small farmers and ordinary people. He envisioned the United States as a republic of free people different from imperialistic nations such as Great Britain.

concern was not the massive plot of extremely cheap land, but the port city that it included—New Orleans. Jefferson recognized the importance of New Orleans for trade and feared French and Spanish interference there. During his presidency, Jefferson reduced the national debt and took many measures to make the young United States a stronger, more independent nation.

The War of 1812

In 1809, James Madison was elected president. Madison had a difficult presidency because so much of his time was spent dealing with the War of 1812.

The Federalists were opposed to the War of 1812 because they saw no profit in it. The British blockade during the war was extremely bad for business in New England, home to many of the Federalists' leaders. The Federalists even went so far as to convene "The Hartford Convention," where they considered the possibility of secession from the Union.

The timing of their convention could not have been worse: days before the Federalists brought word of their convention to Congress, word had already

President James Madison won political favor when the United States won the War of 1812.

arrived that the war was over. Victory was not conclusive for either side, but the Americans won the final battle of the war in the morale-boosting victory of the Battle of New Orleans. The Feder-

Much of the War of 1812 was fought at sea.

alists looked cowardly and unfaithful to the Union. Their image was ruined, and their party never fully recovered from this blow.

The Monroe Doctrine

The period from 1817 to 1825, the presidency of James Monroe, is known as the "Era of Good Feelings." This is partially because of the decline of bipartisan (two-party system) politics. The War of 1812 had inspired a wave of national pride and an increased sense of American identity. In addition, British blockades during the war had forced the American economy to become more self-reliant, and this strengthened trade relations within the nation. The Federalist Party had practically disappeared, and Americans were united by a sense of common identity.

In 1823, Monroe delivered his famous address, called the Monroe Doctrine, to Congress. It declared that America should be free from European interference, and that any new European colonies established in the Americas would be considered as hostile acts. The Monroe Doctrine created the political foundation for the increasingly powerful nation's future identity.

James Monroe's presidency was a period of political peace and harmony.

The Democratic-Republican Party now had no outside enemy to fight. Instead, states began to form their own versions of the Democratic-Republicans, based on the interests and concerns particular to their regions. These differences would eventually tear the party apart.

James Monroe laid the foundation for modern American political thought by issuing the Monroe Doctrine, which stated that Europe had no business interfering in North or South America.

The Whigs

John Quincy Adams and his followers formed a new party called the "National Republicans," later known as the "Whigs." In 1824, Adams was elected president in a close presidential race. Other candidates included Andrew

John Quincy Adam's presidency was a victim of politics: although he was a fair and honest president, the public did not like him, and disagreements within Congress kept him from being able to accomplish much during his time in office.

Jackson and Henry Clay. The polls were so evenly divided between Adams and Jackson that the election came down to a vote in the House of Representatives; Adams won with the support of Henry Clay, who had the most influence in the House. In return for his support, Adams appointed Clay as Secretary of State in what became known as the "Corrupt Bargain."

For the most part, however, John Quincy Adams served honestly and without corruption. Political disagreements in Congress made it difficult for him to accomplish anything during his presidency, though, and his cold and reserved personality did not win him favor with the public.

Andrew Jackson

In 1829, Andrew Jackson was elected president under the newly formed Democratic Party, which emerged from the Democratic–Republican party. Jackson was popular with the working class and with small farmers, not the elite, and he was voted into office by an overwhelming majority of voters.

That same year, Henry Clay focused the spirit of American nationalism into an economic policy called the "American System." The system proposed a new national bank, internal improvements like canals and roads, high prices for public land sold under the Northwest Ordinance, and a high tariff (a tax on imported goods) to protect American industry from foreign competition.

Southerners, however, wanted lower tariff rates because they were heavily involved with trade overseas. They imported manufactured goods and exported massive quantities of tobacco and cotton. In 1833, a compromise tariff was passed in order to resolve a battle between South Carolina and the federal government. Although the federal government did not grant South Carolina all that it wanted, it did give them a fair compromise, proving that states could exert influence against the power of federal government. States' rights continued to be a central political issue throughout the 1800s.

Andrew Jackson was a popular American president, who was often seen as a hero because he had led the American army to victory at the Battle of New Orleans. Many historians look back at Jackson a little differently: Jackson also launched an unauthorized invasion of Florida; Jackson, the great champion of the ordinary white man, owned more than a hundred black Americans; and Jackson expanded the United States by sending thousands of Native Americans on the deadly Trail of Tears that took them from their homes.

SNAPSHOT FROM THE PAST

The Growth of Democracy

Henry H. Thomas turned fourteen years old in 1829, the year Andrew Jackson was elected President. The year before, in 1828, Henry and his family—his mother, father, and two little sisters—had packed up all their belongings and made the long journey from Massachusetts to a small plot of land in Tennessee, where Henry's father used his savings to buy a herd of sheep and enter the spring lamb market.

"This is the best day of my life," Henry's father said on the day they got word of Jackson's election. "I'm proud to have helped elect a man like Jackson."

This was the first time Henry's father had voted. When he had lived on their small farm outside of Boston, Henry's father was excluded from voting because he didn't make enough money or own enough land. He had always been complaining about the bankers in Boston and New York City who controlled the politics in Washington. All that had changed when they moved to Tennessee, where all white men with property (of any size) could vote.

"Out here, in the West," Henry's father told him, "we need a President who believes the same things we do—that every working man is equal to every other working man. And when you grow up, Henry, you'll have a voice in this government too. You'll be able to vote like me."

"What about me?" asked Henry's little sister Jane. "Will I be able to vote when I grow up?"

"Nope." Henry laughed and pulled Jane's pigtail. "Girls don't vote, silly. Just men."

Henry's father would have voted by placing a paper ballot in a box like this.

Jacksonian Democracy

The presidents who came after Andrew Jackson fell in line with a form of politics that came to be known as Jacksonian Democracy. These presidents included Martin Van Buren (Jackson's vice president), John Tyler, and James Polk, "Jacksonians" who supported four central political beliefs:

- extended suffrage—the belief that ordinary white men should be able to vote, regardless of how wealthy they were or how much property they owned.

- strict constructionism—the belief that a federal government should limit its powers and uphold states' rights.

- laissez-faire economics—the belief that the federal government should let the market take care of itself without government regulation or other interference.

- Manifest Destiny—the belief that the United States had a God-given "destiny" to expand westward and populate the entire continent of North America.

This painting portrays the concept of Manifest Destiny—the belief that it was the Divine plan for Americans to spread across the entire North American continent.

EYEWITNESS ACCOUNT

Baltimore, March 1, 1834

The word politics cannot have the same meaning in the United States as in Europe. The United States, are not engaged, like the nations of Europe, in territorial combinations and the preservation of the balance of a continent, nor are they entangled in treaties of Westphalia or Vienna. They are free from all those difficulties, which in Europe arise from a difference of origin or religion, or from the conflict between rival pretensions, between old interests and new interests. They have no neighbor, which excites their suspicions. The policy of the United States consists in the extension of their commerce, and the occupation by agriculture of the vast domain, which nature has given them; in these points is involved the great mass of their general and individual interests; these are the objects which inflame their political and individual passions. As the Banks are the soul of their commerce, their rising manufactures, and even their agriculture, it is evident that the success of their politics is intimately and directly connected with the right organization of their banking system….As among a military people the office of marshal or lord-high-constable is the first in the kingdom, so among a people which, has nothing to do with war, and has only to employ itself with its industry, that of President of the central bank, for example, ought to be a public charge, political, in the sense adapted to the condition and wants of that people—and one of the first rank in the country…

(Excerpt from "Progress of the Struggle—New Powers," a letter in Society, Manners and Politics in the United States; Being a Series of Letters on North America, by Michel Chevalier.)

SNAPSHOT FROM THE PAST

The Freedom to Vote

John Metoyer was born to free black parents in 1833 on a small farm in New York. John's parents had been slaves on a Louisiana sugar plantation when they were bought by a free black family called the Metoyers. The Metoyers had given them their last name and set them free. Not wanting to risk being captured and enslaved again, John's family had headed north, hoping to be left alone for good.

There were no other black families in the surrounding area where the Metoyers lived. No one bothered the Metoyers, but no one talked to them much

Even in the North, free blacks like the Metoyers lived in fear that slave catchers would kidnap them and return them to the South.

either. John's parents never even considered that he would attend the local school. It was always understood that he would stay home and work on the farm.

John's parents never voted during elections. Although they were free, they had no paperwork or proof from their previous owners that proved this fact. They lived in fear that one day slave catchers might arrive at their farm.

But John was a different story, because John had been born in freedom. Ever since 1811, New York State had declared persons like John to be able to vote if they had the paperwork to prove their freedom. When John was born, his parents made sure to register his birth with the local legal system, in order to secure his voting rights. His parents had to appear at court, along with a few of their kinder neighbors who were willing to verify that John (and his family) were not slaves. John grew up knowing that one day he would be able to vote in the State of New York.

Part II
Preserving the Union:
1850–1865

1837

1837 Martin Van Buren becomes the eighth President of the United States.

1838

1838 Trail of Tears—General Winfield Scott and 7,000 troops force Cherokees to walk from Georgia to a reservation set up for them in Oklahoma (nearly 1,000 miles). Around 4,000 Native Americans die during the journey.

1839

1839 The first camera is patented by Louis Daguerre.

1841

1841 William Henry Harrison is elected as the ninth President.

1841 John Tyler becomes the tenth President.

1850

1850 Millard Fillmore becomes the thirteenth President after Taylor dies of a stomach disease.

1850 The Compromise of 1850 confines slavery to the South.

1854

1854 Kansas-Nebraska Act—states that each new state entering the country will decide for themselves whether or not to allow slavery. This goes directly against the terms agreed upon in the Missouri Compromise of 1820.

1857

1857 James Buchanan becomes the fifteenth U.S. President.

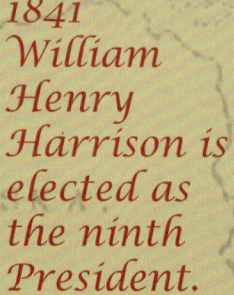

1844

1844 First public telegraph line in the world is opened—between Baltimore and Washington.

1845

1845 James K. Polk becomes the eleventh President.

1848

1848 Seneca Falls Convention—Feminist convention held for women's suffrage and equal legal rights.

1848(-58) California Gold Rush—Over 300,000 people flock to California in search of gold.

1849

1849 Zachary Taylor is elected as the twelfth President.

of the 1800s

1861

1861 Abraham Lincoln begins serving as the sixteenth President.

1861(-65) Civil War—Fought between the Union and Confederate states.

1862

1862 Emancipation Proclamation—Lincoln states that all slaves in Union states are to be freed.

1865

1865 Thirteenth Amendment to the United States Constitution—Officially abolishes slavery across the country.

1865 President Abraham Lincoln is assassinated on April 15.

1865 Andrew Johnson becomes the seventeenth President.

The Compromise of 1850

In 1850, Vice President Millard Fillmore was sworn in as President after Zachary Taylor died in office of a stomach disease. Both Taylor and Fillmore had been elected under the Whig Party. The Whigs favored making Congress more powerful than the executive branch; they also supported modernization programs and economic policies that benefited manufacturing in the North. However, more and more the Whig party was split along pro- and anti-slavery lines.

The South's economy was built on plantations like this one—and plantations could not exist without slave labor.

The Compromise of 1850 offered something to both sides, postponing the inevitable war that was brewing. This gave the North ten more years to industrialize (develop modern factories) and build their infrastructure (railroads for carrying equipment and men.) According to the terms of the compromise:

- California entered the Union as a free state.

- New Mexico and Utah were each allowed to use popular sovereignty to decide the issue of slavery. In other words, the people would pick whether the states would be free or slave.

- The Republic of Texas gave up lands that it claimed in present-day New Mexico and received $10 million to pay its debt to Mexico.

- The slave trade was abolished in the District of Columbia.

- The Fugitive Slave Act made any federal official who did not arrest a runaway slave liable to pay a fine. This was the most controversial part of the Compromise of 1850 and caused many abolitionists to increase their efforts against slavery

Political success during this time was largely based on wealth. Since the Revolutionary War, the South had dominated America's wealth production, and thirteen of the first sixteen American presidents were from slave-holding states (even though the South had fewer voters than the North). The South's cash crops—first tobacco, then cotton—accounted for the vast majority of all American exports.

As the century wore on, however, the South's economic system became increasingly shaky. The South's primary economic goal was protective—to keep slavery in place and allow large-scale farming to continue—while the North's economic goals were spread across many industries. The increasing power and wealth of the Northern states now made it difficult for the South to win political battles in Congress.

Growing Conflicts

During the 1800s, Five Points, an area of Manhattan that is now part of Chinatown, was a dangerous slum. Corrupt politicians took advantage of the residents' poverty. In one election, for example, the number of ballots received from Five Points was higher than the number of actual registered voters in the area at the time.

There were other conflicts besides North and South, Whig and Democrat. In the North, people were divided between ethnic lines. New waves of immigrants from Ireland and Germany threatened the political power of established families. Many of the new immigrants settled in the cities of the Eastern seaboard. The newly arrived were often very poor, especially many Irish who had been forced from their home because of famine. This made them vulnerable to manipulation by corrupt politicians seeking to use their vote to their own benefit. A famous example of an immigrant community torn apart by violence and political corruption was the Five Points neighborhood of lower Manhattan in New York City.

However, the nation as a whole was consumed with issues to the West. A series of conflicts in the 1850s set the stage for the Civil War. The first of these conflicts arose in 1854 from the seemingly harmless goal of opening a transcontinental railway. Stephen A.

During the middle of the nineteenth century, few political issues were not connected to slavery in some way. Even the new concept of a railroad line that crossed the continent was fraught with political tension and resulted in a power struggle that further fueled the growing flames of war.

Douglas, a senator from Illinois, wanted the railroad to run through his state's foremost city, Chicago, but he knew this would anger Southern states, who wanted the railroad to run through the South. So Douglas proposed the Kansas-Nebraska Act, which opened the territories of Kansas and Nebraska for settlement—and Douglas proposed that the issue of slavery in these future states be settled by the voters. The North, however, saw the act as a defeat of their interests, and the Republican Party was created to represent Northern interests.

This drawing shows the white men of Kansas lined up to vote for or against slavery. The Free Soiler Party ultimately won. The main purpose of this political party was opposing the expansion of slavery into the Western territories, arguing that free men on free soil was a morally and economically superior system to slavery.

Bleeding Kansas

The Kansas-Nebraska Act began a race to the newly-opened territory of Kansas. Kansas became the political (and actual) battleground for pro- and anti-slavery groups to wage their war. Both proslavery and "Free-Soil" (anti-slavery) groups rallied people to move to Kansas and settle there, with the hope that their side would be the majority that established a state legislature supporting their view on slavery. Tensions were so high as forces from both sides launched attacks on one another that the territory was called "Bleeding Kansas." In one sense, the Civil War began in Kansas in 1854 and continued into 1859, by which time the Free-Soilers had won the majority in Kansas and elected their own government.

The Dred Scott Decision

Another event that increased tensions between North and South was the Dred Scott Decision of 1857. This was a legal case brought before the Supreme Court in which an African American slave, Dred Scott, sued for his freedom based on his time spent in free states and the recent death of his owner. The Supreme Court ruled against Scott. It declared that any person of African descent in the United States that had been brought here as slave was not protected by the Constitution and could never be. This included the children of slaves as well.

The ruling caused an immediate cry of protest from the North. The North saw it as a threat to the idea of popular sovereignty (which meant white men could vote for or against slavery) in the new territories. If the Dred Scott Decision effectively said, "once a slave, always a slave," then how could new territories ever truly be "free" states?

Things finally came to a head in the presidential election of 1860. The Democrats were divided on the issue of slavery, and being unable to resolve their differences, they split into Northern and Southern parties. John C. Breckinridge represented the Southern Democrats, and Stephen A. Douglas represented

THE POLITICAL QUADRILLE
Music by Dred Scott

This political cartoon portrays the influence of the Dred Scott decision during the 1860 presidential race. Dred Scott is fiddling on a chair at the center, while the candidates "dance" around him. In the upper left is Southern Democrat John C. Breckinridge paired with Democratic incumbent and ally James Buchanan, depicted as a goat (his nickname was "Buck"). At the upper right, Republican Abraham Lincoln prances arm-in-arm with a black woman, a reference to his party's sympathy for the abolitionists. At the lower right, Constitutional Union party candidate John Bell dances with an Indian brave, alluding to Bell's interest in Native Americans. At the lower left, Stephen Douglas dances with a ragged Irishman, referring to his backing among Irish immigrants.

the Northern Democrats. This move weakened the Democrats and made it easier for Abraham Lincoln, the nomi-

The thousands of lives lost during the Civil War was the cost of the unresolved political tension over slavery and states' rights.

nee of the Republican Party, to steal the election. He did so without winning a single Southern state.

A Country at War

In December of 1860, when the votes were counted and the election was final, South Carolina seceded from the Union. Two months later, in February, Mississippi, Florida, Alabama, Georgia, Louisiana, and Texas did the same, forming a new government called the Confederacy. The stage was now set for the Civil War.

Legally, the war began as a response to secession. Lincoln considered the secession of the Southern states an act of rebellion. Although a major outcome of the war was the Emancipation Proclamation (declaring all slaves free), the first goal of the Northern leaders was not the abolition of slavery but the restoration of the Union.

The war was fought mostly on Southern soil, but it took the lives of hundreds of thousands on each side. Eventually, the North's superior supplies and numbers won the day, and the war ended in 1865. The political consequences of the war, however, had only just begun.

INCREDIBLE INDIVIDUAL
Harriet Beecher Stowe

Born in 1811 in Litchfield, Connecticut, Harriet Beecher Stowe is mostly remembered for her novel *Uncle Tom's Cabin* about life for African Americans under slavery.

Harriet was the daughter of a fiery religious leader, Lyman Beecher, and Roxana Foote, a deeply religious woman who died when Harriet was only four years old. Harriet pursued higher education at a seminary run by her older sister Catharine. A few years later, she moved to Cincinnati, Ohio, to be near her father, who had taken a position there as president of Lane Theological Seminary. There she married Calvin Ellis Stowe, a professor and outspoken opponent of slavery. While living in Ohio, Harriet and Calvin supported the Underground Railroad, a system for secretly helping escaped slaves. Eventually, Harriet and Calvin moved back east to Brunswick, Maine, where he took a position at Bowdoin College and she stayed busy raising their seven children.

It was while living in Brunswick and raising her seven children that Harriet wrote the novel for which she is most remembered today. In 1850, Congress passed the Fugitive Slave Law, stating that it was illegal to assist escaped slaves, and this law prompted her to write *Uncle Tom's Cabin*, an account of life under slavery for African Americans. The book, which was first published in installments in the antislavery journal *National Era*, was one of the first pieces of literature to paint the realities of slavery for a national audience. It excited an increase in antislavery attitudes in the North and widespread anger in the South.

The book sold roughly 300,000 copies between 1852 and 1853 alone. It was translated into multiple languages, and had a radical effect on politics in both the United States and Europe. The book was so powerful in the fight against slavery that upon meeting Harriet, Abraham Lincoln is rumored to have said, "So you're the little lady who started this great war!"

EYEWITNESS ACCOUNT

Anita Dwyer Withers, from a diary of her experiences during the Civil War in Richmond, Virginia

April 1st. 1865:

Saturday—A pleasant day. I exchanged nurses, I got Mary Keane from the sisters of Charity.

The 2nd. Sunday we went to Church, the Capt. went to Mr. Grant's farm afterwards. About two o'clock in the day Mr. Myers came around to Mrs. Nelson to inform the Capt. that Richmond was to be evacuated that afternoon.

Gen. Lee telegraphed Mr. Davis that the Yankees had broken through his lines in two different places and he feared would be compelled to give up Richmond & Petersburg.

My Husband did not return from the country until about 5.30, he left me about half past seven.

The President, Cabinet and all the officers belonging to the different departments started on the Cars for Danville, Va. expecting to remain some there and defend that country. My Husband sometimes advised me to go to North Carolina or some other part of the Confederacy, but I refused, believing it best to remain in Richmond, thinking it would be the easiest way I could reach my home.

I never spent two such nights in my life as I did the one of the evacuation and the one following, such fright, anxiety and dread I never before experienced. I felt sick for a week afterwards.

Part III
Reconstruction and the Gilded Age: 1865–1900

1867

1867 United States purchases Alaska from Russia.

1868

1868 Fourteenth Amendment grants blacks equal rights.

1869

1869 Transcontinental Railroad completed on May 10.

1869 Ulysses S. Grant is the eighteenth President.

Time Line

1881

1881 James A. Garfield becomes the twentieth President.

1881 Chester A. Arthur is the twenty-first U.S. President.

1885

1885 Grover Cleveland becomes the twenty-second President.

1886

1886 The Statue of Liberty is dedicated on October 28.

1890

1890 Wounded Knee Massacre— Last battle in the American Indian Wars.

1870

1870 Fifteenth Amendment to the United States Constitution—Prohibits any citizen from being denied to vote based on their "race, color, or previous condition of servitude."

1876

1876 Alexander Graham Bell invents the telephone.

1877

1877 Great Railroad Strike—Often considered the country's first nationwide labor strike.

1877 Rutherford B. Hayes becomes the nineteenth President.

1878

1878 Thomas Edison patents the phonograph on February 19.

1878 Thomas Edison invents the light bulb on October 22.

1892

1892 Ellis Island is opened to receive immigrants coming into New York.

1896

1896 Plessy vs. Ferguson—Supreme Court case that rules that racial segregation is legal as long as accommodations are kept equal.

1896 Henry Ford builds his first combustion-powered vehicle, which he names the Ford Quadricycle.

1897

1897 William McKinley becomes the twenty-fifth President.

1898

1898 The Spanish-American War—The United States gains control of Cuba, Puerto Rico, and the Philippines.

Reconstruction

The years immediately following the Civil War are known as the Reconstruction years because this was the period when the country began the slow and difficult task of putting itself back together. Politically, this meant rebuilding the South while keeping a close eye on it to be sure it was no longer a threat.

During the war, Lincoln took several measures—including the Emancipation Proclamation and the creation of the Freedman's Bureau—that laid the groundwork for the future of African Americans. But the abolition of slavery combined with the war's devastation meant that the South's economy was nonexistent.

If Lincoln had been able to lead the Reconstruction, it might have gone differently. But Lincoln was assassinated, and his vice president, Andrew Johnson, was left with the overwhelming task of healing a nation. Johnson's poli-

President Lincoln was assassinated by John Wilkes Booth on April 14, 1865, while the President, his wife, and two guests were attending the theater. Booth and his co-conspirators were Confederate sympathizers who had originally planned to kill the Vice President and the Secretary of State as well.

EYEWITNESS ACCOUNT

Excerpt from Letters to the Connecticut Courant, Pennsylvania Republican, Washington Chronicle, North Carolina Union Banner, Nemaha Courier, Pittsburgh Commercial and Topeka Record, by D. F. Drinkwater.

Washington, December 7, 1866

The breach between the President and the people's Representatives is, if possible, wider than ever, and no one will deny that the Executive and Legislative branches of the Government are in direct antagonism. At the last session Congress was reasonably conciliatory to Mr. Johnson, and hesitated to adopt any measures looking towards aggravating the unhappy differences. I say reasonably conciliatory; perhaps unreasonably is the right word. Since the adjournment last July, events have transpired which remove all possible doubts about the stubbornness of the recreant Chief Magistrate, his sympathy with treason and traitors and his persistent and unchangeable efforts to do all in his power against the loyal and for the disloyal. Congress understands the situation and if speeches mean anything will act accordingly. "Acts" are wanted, however, speeches are of little practical good, unless their utterances are carried out.

. . . You know how Congress failed in many promised things last session, let us hope for greater earnestness this time.

Yours truly,

D. F. Drinkwater.

cies toward the South were considered to be too soft, and his hurry to let the former Confederate states back into the Union earned him the wrath of his political opponents. When he vetoed civil rights bills, the Republicans were furious. By 1866, the Radical Republicans had gained control of Congress, and Johnson's control of Reconstruction came to an end.

Carpetbaggers and Scalawags

A major part of Reconstruction was sending Northerners to the South to take political and government offices. Northern whites arriving in the South to take political positions were known as "Carpetbaggers," an insult that compared the newly arrived Northerners to homeless persons who packed all their belongings into large carpetbags.

Under the control of the newly arrived politicians, the Southern states were forced to ratify the Fourteenth Amendment, giving African Americans citizenship. A flurry of other civil rights laws were passed in the years that followed: the Civil Rights Act of 1866 (giving all black males the same citizenship rights as white males), the Fifteenth Amendment of 1870 (giving African Americans the right to vote in elections), and finally the Civil Rights Act of 1875 (giving all people the right to public places regardless of race or previous servitude).

Also during this time, Congress attempted to prepare for the eventual transfer of government power back to Southerners. Unfortunately, the period of Reconstruction failed to put in place structures and systems that would provide continued protection to African Americans in the south. When President Rutherford B. Hayes finally pulled the Army out of the last three Southern states, the brief period of civil rights for African Americans had come to a close, and racism flourished through the end of the 1800s.

In the North, blacks faced rising competition for jobs and the struggle

Carpetbaggers were seen as interfering Northern outsiders with questionable objectives meddling in local politics, buying up plantations at rock-bottom prices, taking advantage of poor Southerners, and pushing their alien Northern ways on Southern politics.

EXTRA! EXTRA!

Daily Oklahoma, February 22, 1873
Editorial: Give Justice to Both Races
Negro Must be Made to Know His Place—
Should Have Equal Privileges But Entirely Separate

Give the negro a chance by making him understand that a line must be drawn between the white and black races.

Educate him in a school that is presided over by negroes and whose pupils are all negroes.

Give entirely equal advantage of railway passenger facilities but separate him from white passengers.

Provide a waiting room for him at every railway station in the new state, and make all appointments equally as good as those given to the white race.

Permit him to better his moral and financial condition, but let him realize always that

Have YOU a Daughter, Mr. Voter

he must not hope for social equity with the white man.

This is my attitude toward the negro.

for land and resources. In the South, whites held the power and used systems like the Jim Crow Laws to keep African Americans out of the voting booth. Blacks lived in constant danger in the years following the Civil War, but there was no more dangerous time than election time, when groups of whites attacked, intimidated, and even murdered African Americans who voted Republican. White Southerners who supported the Republican Party were labeled "Scalawags" and were also harassed.

INCREDIBLE INDIVIDUAL
Frederick Douglass

Frederick Douglass was born a slave, so no one knows for sure when he was born—probably somewhere around 1818. When he was about twelve, his owner's wife Sophia began to teach him the alphabet. She was breaking the law by teaching a slave to read, and when her husband discovered what she was doing, he forced her to stop. The seed had been planted in Frederick's mind, however, and in the years that followed he did everything in his power to continue his education. He learned what he could from the white children in his neighborhood and soon was reading everything he could put his hands on—newspapers, magazines, books of every size and subject. When he was an older boy, he taught other slaves how to read the New Testament of the Bible at weekly Sunday school sessions. When his white owners found out, they put an end to his lessons. Douglass tried many times to escape and failed each time until 1837, when he successfully made it to New York City.

There, Douglass immediately began a life of faithful advocacy for his fellow African Americans. He was one of the first public figures to disprove the lie that African Americans were somehow less intelligent than whites, for he was living proof that African Americans were intelligent, capable, and respectable. Douglass published numerous magazines with abolitionist messages. The motto of one of his publications, called *The North Star*, was "Right is of no Sex, Truth is of no Color, God is the Father of us all, and we are all brethren."

Douglass's work took him all over the world. He gave a series of lectures in England that earned him enormous respect there, where the abolition of slavery throughout the British Empire was being argued. He served in U.S. politics as ambassador to Haiti and as head of the Reconstruction-era Freedman's Federal Reserve Bank. He was even nominated as Vice President to an extremely controversial party called the Equal Rights Party—a nomination that Douglass never officially acknowledged.

His life's work was not confined merely to the rights of black Americans but to all people. Douglass spoke at many women's rights meetings and was a frequent spokesman for the cause of Native Americans. He believed that education was fundamental to helping the powerless help themselves, and that belief became the backbone of his life's work. He often said, "I would unite with anybody to do right and with nobody to do wrong."

The Gilded Age

Author Mark Twain used the term "the Gilded Age" to describe the years after the Civil War. The word "gilded" means to cover something with a thin layer of gold. The authors chose "Gilded Age" as a play-on-words for "Golden Age"—meaning the wealth and prosperity of America in those years only appeared to be golden. Actually, only a very few Americans achieved great wealth in those gilded years. With the massive growth of industry in the United States came a massive influx of money—but not everyone benefited.

A political cartoon portrays the way big business profited during the Gilded Age, growing fat on the profits generated from Reconstruction.

Corrupt politics helped to make the rich richer and the poor poorer. In the cities, what were called "political machines" became the dominant force in politics. These political machines elected officials based on their willingness to act on the behalf of the wealthy men who helped elect them. They offered rewards to voters and used violence and crime to enforce their will.

Even during the Gilded Age's years of corruption, the American ideal of equality for all still remained alive, as shown in this political cartoon portraying all different kinds of people sitting down together to Thanksgiving Dinner.

Corruption existed at the federal level as well. The presidency of Ulysses S. Grant following the war is said to have been one of the most corrupt in all of U.S. history. A "spoils system" emerged in politics, whereby local, state, and national government jobs were given to supporters of a political party if its candidate won an election. Money, power, and politics began to mix too easily, and in the process, elections became based more on personality and less on political issues. This is the period when "mudslinging" first became popular. Mudslinging meant that each candidate attacked their opponent's character and made often false accusations in order to get an advantage at the polls.

After the Civil War was over, many Americans viewed Ulysses S. Grant with approval because of the role he had played in bringing victory to the North. This image from the cover of Harper's Weekly portrays Grant as freedom's hero. This tide of feeling was what elected Grant to the presidency.

Corruption in the U.S. government during Grant's presidency extended to many issues, including the unfair treatment of Native tribes. This political cartoon from a newspaper shows Grant with the Interior Secretary hiding behind him, facing Red Cloud, Chief of the Oglala Sioux. The Secretary of the Interior is extending his arms, pretending to be Grant, offering a handful of cheap cooking utensils as he presents a receipt that reads, "Recd. for Black Hills $25,000 in 'Goods'" to Red Cloud, asking him to make his mark. Red Cloud replies, "Never!"

END OF THE BIG TALK AT WASHINGTON.
THE GREAT FATHER—"*Set your mark there, and 'twill be all right.*"
RED CLOUD (seeing Delano behind the President)—"*Never—except for cash !*"

"Waving the bloody shirt" was another popular practice amongst politicians of the time. Politicians from the North and South used memories of the Civil War to stir up opposition to the other side. Corrupt politicians from the Republican Party, which had carried the North through the Civil War, were especially effective at "waving the red flag." They constantly reminded Northern voters that the Democrats had been responsible for the South's rebellion.

The South became the "Solid South" during post-Civil War years, almost always voting Democratic. They weren't able to elect a Democratic president, however, until the 1884 election of Grover Cleveland. Even this was only possible because corruption amongst the Republicans (beginning with Ulysses S. Grant's presidency) had caused a group of reformers called the Mugwumps to split off, dividing the vote. (The word "mugwump" comes from an Algonquian Native word that meant "important person.")

INCREDIBLE INDIVIDUAL
Ulysses S. Grant

When Ulysses S. Grant was elected president, the American people hoped for an end to turmoil. Grant, however, did not give them what they had hoped for. Looking to Congress for direction, he seemed bewildered. One visitor to the White House noted "a puzzled pathos, as of a man with a problem before him of which he does not understand the terms."

As the Union general during the Civil War, Grant had helped bring an end to a long and bloody war. A grateful nation saw him as a hero who would bring the same decisive courage to the White House. A clever general, however, does not translate into a wise President. As President, Grant presided over the U.S. government much as he had run the Army. He even brought part of his Army staff to the White House.

Although a man of scrupulous honesty, Grant as President accepted generous presents from admirers. Worse, he allowed himself to be associated with two speculators, Jay Gould and James Fisk. When Grant realized their scheme to corner the market in gold, he authorized the Secretary of the Treasury to sell enough gold to wreck their plans, but the speculation had already wrought havoc with business.

During his campaign for re-election in 1872, Grant was attacked by Liberal Republican reformers. He called them "narrow-headed men," their eyes so close together that "they can look out of the same gimlet hole without winking." Meanwhile, the General's friends in the Republican Party came to be known proudly as "the Old Guard." Grant allowed Radical Reconstruction to run its course in the South, bolstering it at times with military force.

Grant's reputation suffered through no fewer than twelve political scandals during the years of his presidency. His reactions to the scandals ranged from prosecuting the perpetrators to protecting or pardoning those who were accused and convicted of the crimes. When the Whiskey Ring scandal broke out in 1875, Grant, in a reforming mood, wrote, "Let no guilty man escape." However, when it was found out that his personal secretary Orville E. Babcock was indicted, Grant testified on behalf of the defendant. When Secretary of War William W. Belknap was involved in a trading-post extortion scam, Grant promptly accepted his resignation without question, and then went to a photography studio to get his portrait done. In essence, when it came to prosecuting those guilty of graft, Grant used his presidential power to protect close friends, particularly his military associates.

After leaving the presidency, Grant became a partner in a financial firm, which went bankrupt. About that time, he learned that he had cancer of the throat. He started writing his memories to pay off his debts and provide for his family, racing against death to produce a memoir that ultimately earned nearly $450,000. Soon after completing the last page, in 1885, he died.

The End of the Century

During the last years of the nineteenth century, the trend of ordinary people being involved in politics, which had begun during Andrew Jackson's presidency, continued to increase. Americans of all sorts began to associate themselves with particular parties, the largest of which were the Republicans and the Democrats. Never before had politicians used such emotional rallies to stir voters towards one party or away from another. Nearly 80 percent of eligible Americans took advantage of their right to vote. (So far, in the elections of the twenty-first century, only 60–65 percent of all voters have voted.)

With the massive industrialization of the nation and the ever-expanding development of the West, politics became increasingly money driven,

William Jennings Bryan campaigning for the presidency.

as was seen clearly in the last presidential election of the nineteenth century, in 1896. William McKinley, the Republican candidate, ran against the Democrat William Jennings Bryan, and their campaigns were marked by contrasts. Bryan crisscrossed the country making personal appearances. When he was accused of lacking dignity, he answered, "I would rather have it said that I lacked dignity than that I lacked backbone to meet the enemies of the government who work against its welfare from Wall Street." Meanwhile, McKinley stayed home and ran a front-porch campaign where thousands of people came to his home and heard him speak. Bryan's opponents depicted him as a "radical and socialist," while McKinley's enemies called him a "tool of business." McKinley raised $3 million (mostly from business interests), while Bryan's supporters were only able to raise $600,000. McKinley won the election

During the twentieth century, new issues would confront the United States, as the nation grew increasingly powerful on the world stage. In many ways,

William McKinley.

however, America's political challenges remained the same—as they do even today in the twenty-first century. Since its birth, the United States has felt a continual tension between states' rights and a strong central government, between big business and the rights of ordinary people, and these conflicting points of view continue to shape America. American politics are forged from these opposing perspectives—and the ongoing compromises between the two shape our daily lives.

EYEWITNESS ACCOUNT

by Susan B. Anthony
Pioneer for Women's Rights

Friends and fellow citizens: I stand before you tonight under indictment for the alleged crime of having voted at the last presidential election, without having a lawful right to vote. It shall be my work this evening to prove to you that in thus doing, I not only committed no crime, but, instead, simply exercised my citizen's rights, guaranteed to me and all United States citizens by the National Constitution, beyond the power of any State to deny.

Our democratic-republican government is based on the idea of the natural right of every individual member thereof to a voice and a vote in making and executing the laws. . . . All men are created equal, and endowed by their Creator with certain inalienable rights. Among these are life, liberty and the pursuit of happiness. To secure these, governments are instituted among men, deriving their just powers from the consent of the governed. Here is no shadow of government authority over rights, or exclusion of any class from their full and equal enjoyment. Here is pronounced the right of all men, and "consequently," as the Quaker preacher said, "of all women," to a voice in the government. And here, in this first paragraph of the Declaration, is the assertion of the natural right of all to the ballot; for how can "the consent of the governed" be given, if the right to vote be denied? . . .

The women, dissatisfied as they are with this form of government, that enforces taxation without representation—that compels them to obey laws to which they have never given their consent—that imprisons and hangs them without a trial by a

During the late 1800s, Susan B. Anthony brought another political issue to the American scene— women's rights, including the right to vote.

jury of their peers—that robs them, in marriage, of the custody of their own persons, wages and children—are this half of the people who are left wholly at the mercy of the other half, in direct violation of the spirit and the letter of the declarations of the framers of this government, every one of which was based on the immutable principles of equal rights to all. By these declarations, kings, popes, priests, aristocrats, all were alike dethroned and placed on a common level, politically, with the lowliest born subject or serf. By them, too, men, as such, were deprived of their divine right to rule and placed on a political level with women. By the practice of these declarations all class and caste distinctions would be abolished, and slave, serf, plebeian, wife, woman, all alike rise from their subject position to the broader platform of equality.

The preamble of the Federal Constitution says: We, the people of the United States. . . . It was we, the people; not we, the white male citizens; nor we, the male citizens; but we, the whole people, who formed the Union. And we formed it, not to give the blessings of liberty, but to secure them; not to the half of ourselves and the half of our posterity, but to the whole people —women as well as men. And it is a downright mockery to talk to women of their enjoyment of the blessings of liberty while they are denied the use of the only means of securing them provided by this democratic-republican government —the ballot.

. . . Our government is not a democracy. It is not a republic. It is an odious aristocracy; a hateful oligarchy of sex; the most hateful aristocracy ever established on the face of the globe; an oligarchy of wealth, where the rich govern the poor. An oligarchy of learning, where the educated govern the ignorant, or even an oligarchy of race, where the Saxon rules the African, might be endured; but this oligarchy of sex, which makes father, brothers, husband, sons, the oligarchs over the mother and sisters, the wife and daughters, of every household —which ordains all men sovereigns, all women subjects, carries dissension, discord, and rebellion into every home of the nation.

The only question left to be settled now is: Are women persons? And I hardly believe any of our opponents will have the hardihood to say they are not. Being persons, then, women are citizens; and no state has a right to make any law, or to enforce any old law, that shall abridge their privileges or immunities. Hence, every discrimination against women in the constitutions and laws of the several states is today null and void, precisely as is every one against Negroes.

EXTRA! EXTRA!

From the Sacramento Daily Record Union,
Thursday, January 1, 1880
NEWS OF THE MORNING

Tom Pico, a horse thief, was shot Monday at Riverside, San Bernardino county.

Hon. George S. Houston, United States Senator, died yesterday at Athens, Ga.

The explosion of a giant powder cartridge at Oakland yesterday injured two men, one seriously.

A most wonderful case is reported from Watsonville—the death of a woman who for a quarter of a century passed as a man.

Fred L. Ames has been elected President of the Boston, Hoosac Tunnel and Western Railroad.

Richard Smith, of the Cincinnati Gazette, has been arrested on a charge of criminal libel.

Mrs. Cynthia Hodgdon, the convicted abortionist, has been denied bail in San Francisco.

The Stock Boards adjourned in San Francisco yesterday until Friday.

An accident occurred yesterday on the Chicago, Milwaukee and St. Paul Railway, but without serious results.

At Ottawa, Canada, the thermometer marked 20° below zero.

The new Constitution of Louisiana was adopted by 59,148.

President Grant is receiving a hearty welcome in the South.

Keene has shipped $4,000,000 in gold to Chicago to conduct his January deal in wheat.

A woman near Los Angeles yesterday threw her child into a pool and drowned it.

At Burlington, Ia., yesterday, John A. Woodward shot and killed Edward Price, and then committed suicide.

Buildings were erected at Portland, Or., during 1879 valued at $1,162,700.

This newspaper account of the daily happenings in 1880 reveals a world not so very different from ours today. Disasters were happening; crime was taking place; people were interested in the weather; financial news made headlines; and politicians were attracting attention.

Think About It

In 1800, only a minority of Americans—adult white men who owned property—had the right to vote and elect representatives to government offices. By 1850, the right to vote had been extended to all adult white male citizens and, after the Civil War, to adult African American men, many of whom had been slaves. By 1900 there was a strong movement for women's suffrage (the right to vote).

- How do you think the extension of the right to vote to white men of all classes (not just property owners) changed American politics in the mid-1800s?

- How do you think giving African American men the right to vote might have potentially changed things in the post-Civil War South?

- Voting was considered a right and a privilege in 1800s America. Why do you think so few Americans in the twenty-first century (less than 60% of eligible voters in the last presidential election) exercise that right?

Words Used in This Book

abolitionists: People who believed that slavery should be abolished or done away with.

advocacy: Supporting or arguing for a person, a cause, or an idea.

aristocracy: A group of people with high ranks, titles, and privileges, often passed down through heredity, and, sometimes, a government ruled by such a group.

bipartisan: Including members of two different political parties.

cash crops: Any crop that is grown to be sold directly, instead of being used, for example, as food for livestock.

civil rights: The rights of a person to personal freedoms, given through citizenship.

conciliatory: Something that helps overcome distrust and encourages friendship.

controversial: Having to do with something that people disagree about.

corruption: Dishonesty; often involving dishonest acts such as bribery.

elite: The best of a group, in terms of wealth, social class, skill, or other qualities.

emancipation: The act of setting someone free.

equity: Equality; fair and equal treatment.

evacuation: The removal of people from an area, often to get them away from a dangerous situation.

executive: The branch of the government responsible for making sure the laws are upheld.

extortion: When a person uses his position to get money or privileges.

federal: Referring to the central government uniting a group of smaller state governments.

graft: Getting money or advantages through dishonest means, especially through use of one's political power or position.

inalienable: Absolute, not able to be taken away.

industrialization: The development of industry in an area.

intimidated: Caused fear; used fear to force or prevent some action.

Jim Crow Laws: A group of state and local laws between 1876 and 1965 requiring racial segregation, with "separate but equal" facilities for black people and white people.

laissez-faire: From the French words meaning "to let" and "to do," meaning that the government has nothing to do with making laws about economics.

legislative: The branch of the government responsible for making laws.

nationalism: Being loyal and devoted to one's country, and wanting to help the country expand or advance.

oligarchy: A form of government where a small group rules.

popular sovereignty: When the people of a state or nation have the power to make political decisions and laws or else the elected officials are required to follow the will of the people.

proclamation: An official formal announcement.

radical: Extreme, often going against traditional ways of doing things.

ratify: To confirm by giving formal approval.

Reconstruction: The period after the Civil War when the Confederate states were reorganized, rebuilt, and governed by the federal government.

republic: A form of government in which the people vote for representatives who are then responsible to them for their political decisions and actions.

restoration: The process of repairing something or putting something back to the way it had been originally.

secession: The act of officially withdrawing from an organization, such as a political union.

servitude: Slavery or forced labor.

speculators: Those who take large risks (especially financial) in the hopes of large gains.

tariff: A tax on imported goods.

treason: Disloyalty to one's country, to the extent that a person tries to overthrow or seriously hurt the government, or tries to help the country's enemies succeed.

veto: The power to cancel a decision by another group.

Find Out More

In Books

Conklin, Wendy. *Civil War Leaders: Expanding & Preserving the Union.* Huntington Beach, Calif.: Teacher Created Materials, 2008.

Gunderson, Cory Gideon. *The Dred Scott Decision.* Edina, Minn.: ABDO & Daughters, 2004.

Hale, Sarah Elder, ed. *Rebuilding a Nation: Picking Up the Pieces.* Peterborough, N.H.: Cobblestone, 2005.

King, David C. *Civil War and Reconstruction.* Hoboken, N.J.: Wiley, 2003.

McComb, Marianne. *American Documents: The Emancipation Proclamation.* Margate, Fla.: National Geographic Children's Books, 2005.

Mountjoy, Shane. *Manifest Destiny: Westward Expansion.* New York: Chelsea House, 2009.

Perritano, John. *Graphic America: Radical Republicans.* New York: Crabtree, 2008.

Porterfield, Jason. *Problems and Progress in American Politics: The Growth of the Democratic Party in the Late 1800s.* New York: Rosen, 2003.

Stites, Bill. *The Republican Party in the Late 1800s: A Changing Role for American Government.* New York: Rosen, 2003.

On the Internet

American's Reconstruction: People and Politics After the Civil War
www.digitalhistory.uh.edu/reconstruction/section1/section1_intro.html

Civil War
www.civilwar.com

Kingwood College Library
19th Century
kclibrary.lonestar.edu/19thcentury1800.htm

Manifest Destiny
www.pbs.org/kera/usmexicanwar/prelude/manifest_destiny_overview.html

Teaching American History
Slavery, Ante-Bellum Politics and Westward Expansion
teachingamericanhistory.org/library/index.asp?document=1515

The White House
The Presidents
www.whitehouse.gov/about/presidents

Index

Picture Credits

Abraham Lincoln Presidential Library pp. 22–23
Bowdoin College Museum of Art pp. 16–19
Granger Collection 1pp. 6–17, 30–31
Harper's Weekly pp. 25, 32–33, 36, 46–49
Library of Congress pp. 12–13, 16–17, 20–21, 28–31, 37, 40–55
National Portrait Gallery pp. 34–35
University of North Carolina pp. 34–35
U.S. Government pp. 9, 14–19
Washington University Law School pp. 12–13

To the best knowledge of the publisher, all images not specifically credited are in the public domain. If any image has been inadvertently uncredited, please notify Harding House Publishing Service, 220 Front Street, Vestal, New York 13850, so that credit can be given in future printings.

About the Author and the Consultant

Zachary Chastain is an independent writer and actor living in Binghamton, New York. He is the author of various educational books for both younger and older audiences.

John Gillis is a Rutgers University Professor of History Emeritus. A graduate of Amherst College and Stanford University, he has taught at Stanford, Princeton, University of California at Berkeley, as well as Rutgers. Gillis is well known for his work in social history, including pioneering studies of age relations, marriage, and family. The author or editor of ten books, he has also been a fellow at both St. Antony's College, Oxford, and Clare Hall, Cambridge.